NATIONAL GEOGRAPHIC

Ladders

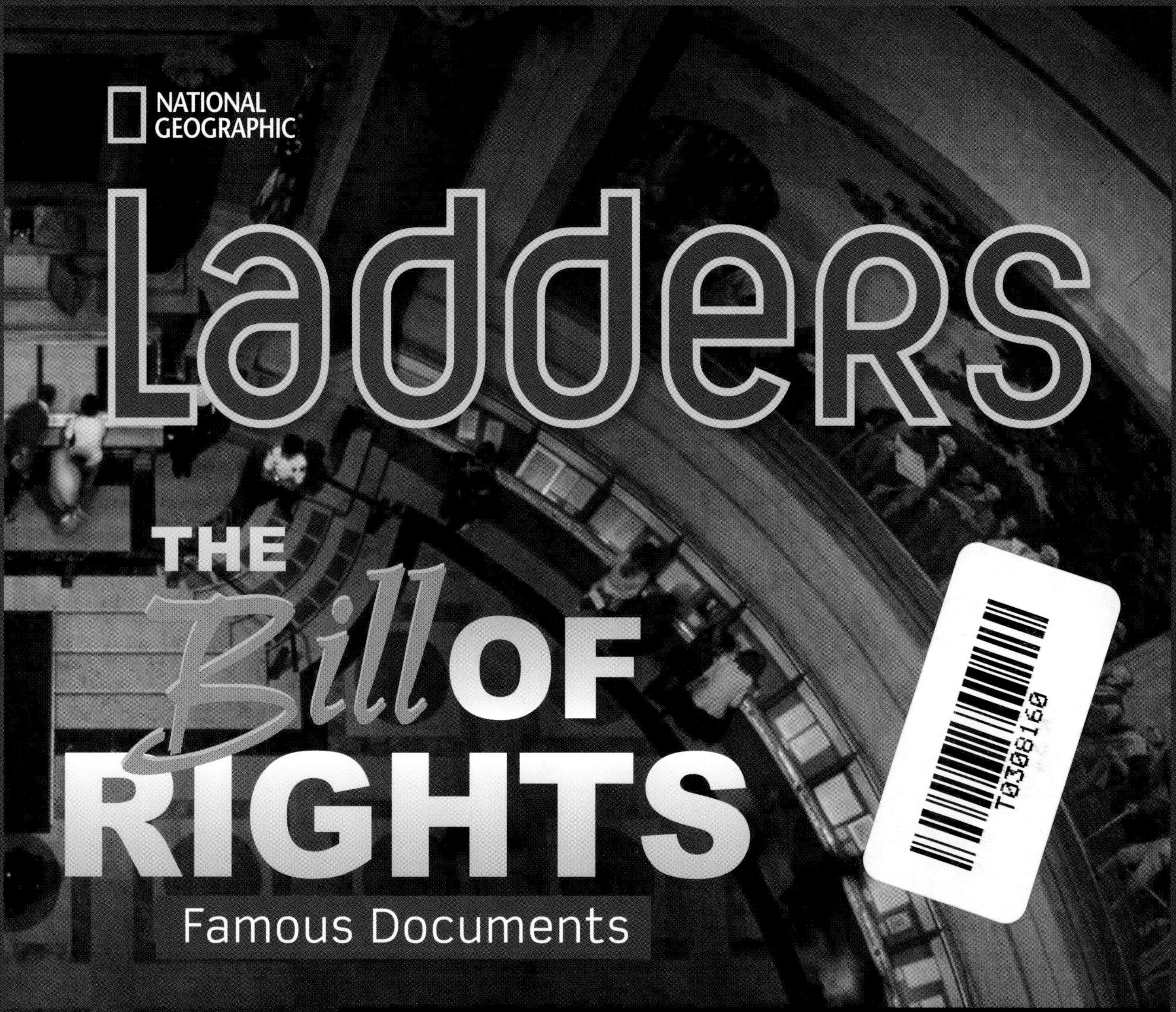

THE Bill OF RIGHTS

Famous Documents

GENRE Reference Article

Read to find out about the Bill of Rights.

Meet the Bill of Rights

by Sheri Reda

Visitors view the Bill of Rights in Washington, D.C. Want a picture of yourself next to the Bill of Rights? You can't take one anymore. You could once. But a camera's flash can harm the document, so taking pictures is no longer allowed.

We Americans are very fortunate. We live in a nation where we can share our opinions openly and without fear of government punishment. We can protest peacefully and ask the legislature to change laws we believe are unfair. Our homes cannot be searched or our property taken away from us without good reason, and we have religious freedom as well. The Bill of Rights guarantees, or formally assures, these basic **rights** and more.

But this wasn't always true. When Britain ruled the American colonies, British officials could arrest colonists just for sharing their opinions and thoughts in public. The colonists also had to put up with being searched, arrested, or even thrown in jail, all for no good reason. Once in jail, they often were kept there for long periods of time. So in 1787, when the Founders of the United States wrote the Constitution, they wanted to make sure that these things never happened to American citizens.

As you know, the Constitution sets out a plan for our government. The Founders approved the plan, but in 1791, they added something important—a Bill of Rights. The ten **amendments**, or changes and additions to the Constitution, that make up the Bill of Rights list our basic rights and safeguard our individual freedoms.

Drumroll, Please

And here they are: *your* basic rights! As old as it is, the Bill of Rights is an ever-changing document that we continue to adjust to make the rights fit the needs of Americans today. Its language may be old-fashioned, but that's the way people spoke and wrote back then. Still, its ideas are timeless.

Amendment I

Congress shall make no law respecting an establishment of religion, or prohibiting the free exercise thereof; or abridging the freedom of speech, or of the press; or the right of the people peaceably to assemble, and to petition the Government for a redress of grievances.

The government can't tell you what to believe, write, or say. People have the right to gather peacefully in public and ask the government to change its policies.

Amendment II

A well-regulated Militia, being necessary to the security of a free State, the right of the people to keep and bear Arms, shall not be infringed.

Americans have the right to own and use weapons to defend themselves.

Amendment III

No Soldier shall, in time of peace be quartered in any house, without the consent of the Owner, nor in time of war, but in a manner to be prescribed by law.

No one can force you to shelter and feed soldiers in your home, as the colonists were forced to do for British soldiers.

Amendment IV

The right of the people to be secure in their persons, houses, papers, and effects, against unreasonable searches and seizures, shall not be violated, and no Warrants shall issue, but upon probable cause, supported by Oath or affirmation, and particularly describing the place to be searched, and the persons or things to be seized.

The police cannot arrest you or search you or your home unless they have a good reason and a judge's permission.

Amendment V

No person shall be held to answer for a capital, or otherwise infamous crime, unless on a presentment or indictment of a Grand Jury, except in cases arising in the land or naval forces, or in the Militia, when in actual service in time of War or public danger; nor shall any person be subject for the same offence to be twice put in jeopardy of life or limb; nor shall be compelled in any criminal case to be a witness against himself, nor be deprived of life, liberty, or property, without due process of law; nor shall private property be taken for public use, without just compensation.

The government cannot send you to prison without a trial, put you on trial twice for the same crime, or force you to give evidence against yourself in court.

Amendment VI

In all criminal prosecutions, the accused shall enjoy the right to a speedy and public trial, by an impartial jury of the State and district wherein the crime shall have been committed, which district shall have been previously ascertained by law, and to be informed of the nature and cause of the accusation; to be confronted with the witnesses against him; to have compulsory process for obtaining witnesses in his favor, and to have the Assistance of Counsel for his defense.

If you are charged with a crime, you have the right to understand what you are being charged with and to face the people who have charged you. You also have a right to a lawyer and a speedy trial.

Amendment VII

In Suits at common law, where the value in controversy shall exceed twenty dollars, the right of trial by jury shall be preserved, and no fact tried by a jury, shall be otherwise re-examined in any Court of the United States, than according to the rules of the common law.

You have the right to be tried by a jury of fellow citizens.

Amendment VIII

Excessive bail shall not be required, nor excessive fines imposed, nor cruel and unusual punishments inflicted.

If you're arrested, you should not have to pay too much money, or bail, so you can be free until trial. You are also safe from cruel and extreme punishment. And you don't have to pay fines that are too high for the crime you may have committed.

Amendment IX

The enumeration in the Constitution, of certain rights, shall not be construed to deny or disparage others retained by the people.

You have other rights and freedoms in addition to the ones listed in the Constitution.

Amendment X

The powers not delegated to the United States by the Constitution, nor prohibited by it to the States, are reserved to the States respectively, or to the people.

Powers not clearly given to the national government by the Constitution belong to the states.

Check In Why was the Bill of Rights created?

GENRE Social Studies Article

Read to find out about the rights protected by the First Amendment.

The 5 FREEDOMS

by Sheri Reda

The first one says it all—almost.

The Constitution's First Amendment contains some of our most important individual freedoms: freedom of religion, speech, press, assembly, and petition. What do all of these freedoms mean, and why were these rights created? How do they affect our lives today? Let's find out by reading some real examples about people's rights before and after the First Amendment was written.

Freedom of Religion

Freedom of religion means the right to worship—or not worship—as you please. It also means that you can't interfere with the religious rights of others. Long before the First Amendment was written, the Puritans came to America from Britain to escape unfair religious treatment and to follow their own religion in peace. In America, though, the Puritans didn't grant the same freedom to others. In the Massachusetts Bay colony, Puritan ministers were outraged when one woman, Anne Hutchinson, criticized their teachings. They put her on trial and found her guilty. Then they made her leave the colony.

Today, the First Amendment protects religious freedom. For example, in 2003, a school in Oklahoma suspended sixth-grader Nashala Hearn for violating its dress code. The school district outlawed the headscarf, or *hijab,* she wore as part of her Muslim faith. Nashala's family sued and won. The Court ordered the district to allow students to wear religious head coverings.

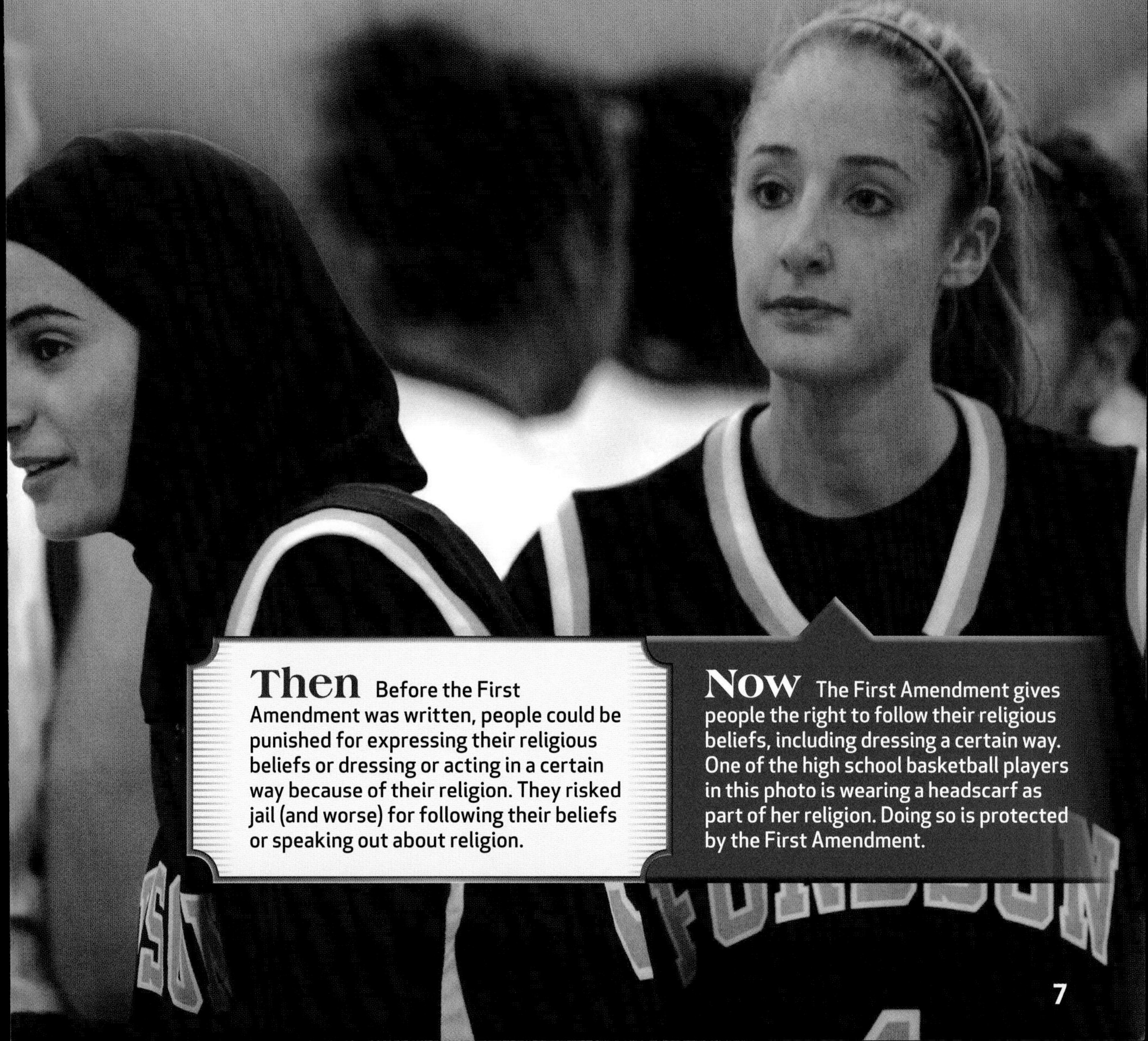

Then Before the First Amendment was written, people could be punished for expressing their religious beliefs or dressing or acting in a certain way because of their religion. They risked jail (and worse) for following their beliefs or speaking out about religion.

Now The First Amendment gives people the right to follow their religious beliefs, including dressing a certain way. One of the high school basketball players in this photo is wearing a headscarf as part of her religion. Doing so is protected by the First Amendment.

Freedom of Speech

Freedom of speech doesn't mean you can say just anything. For example, you can't yell "Fire!" as a joke in a crowded movie theater. That could put peoples' lives in danger. But the First Amendment does guarantee your right to express opinions. And that includes opinions that are critical of the government. That wasn't always allowed. In colonial America, the king's officials limited freedom of speech. Criticizing the British government was a crime. Many colonists were imprisoned for speaking out against the British.

Once the United States won its freedom, the writers of the Bill of Rights made sure to protect the right of free speech in the First Amendment. How can we protect free speech and also protect people from "verbal bullies"? When people post mean things about others on social media sites or bother them through texts or chats, it's called **cyber-bullying**. Today, 49 states have laws against cyber-bullying. The laws are designed to protect people from being attacked online for things such as their race, religion, or age.

Then Colonial Americans could get in big trouble for speaking out, especially against the government.

Now As you can see from the texts on this phone, Evan is a bully. His messages are meant to hurt Alex. Today, cyber-bullying laws try to balance the First Amendment right to free speech with the need to protect people from damaging words like these.

Freedom of the Press

Freedom of the press means that we can print and distribute our ideas, no matter how unpopular they are. Today, we can publish them in everything from newspapers and magazines to Web sites.

People have been fighting for this freedom since the 1700s. In 1734, colonist John Peter Zenger, a printer, published a newspaper called the *Weekly Journal*. He printed articles about the bad deeds of William Cosby, the British colonial governor of New York. Cosby charged Zenger with "seditious libel." He claimed Zenger had printed information that hurt his reputation. Zenger's lawyer argued that Zenger had the right to publish articles about the governor, as long as the information was true. He believed that a charge of libel should only apply to publishing lies. The jury agreed. That gave Zenger and the colonists an important victory in the fight for freedom of the press, nearly 60 years before the First Amendment was even written.

Then When the colonies were governed by the British, you needed a license from the government to print something, and you usually couldn't print anything critical of the government or its officials. However, court victories such as Zenger's (illustrated above) began paving the way toward achieving freedom of the press years later.

Now Reporters exercise freedom of the press by publishing information about sensitive topics. Sometimes their cases end up in the courts, which work to decide how the First Amendment applies to each individual situation.

Right to Assemble

The right to **assemble**, or to meet with others, means that people can hold meetings and gather in public, as long as these assemblies are peaceful and lawful. However, American colonists weren't protected by this right when they wanted to gather to talk about their unfair treatment under British rule. British officials were afraid that the colonists were planning to revolt, so they used troops to break up these meetings. Of course, this only made the colonists more determined to meet. Once they won independence from Great Britain, they made sure to protect everyone's right to assemble under the First Amendment.

In fall of 2011, people of all ages gathered around the United States to **protest** what they saw as the inequality between the lives of the very rich and everyone else. They called their protest the "Occupy Movement" because they occupied, or took over, public spaces in cities around the United States, including New York City. In several states, including Tennessee, these protesters were arrested for violating local curfew laws, which required them to be inside by a certain time. But Tennessee courts said "No." They ruled that the arrests violated the protesters' First Amendment right to assemble.

Then The British found the colonists' assemblies threatening, so they sent troops to break them up, as pictured here. They hoped this would stop people from gathering to protest against the government.

Now The right to assemble protects groups who want to organize and gather. As long as they remain peaceful and don't harm people or property, they are free to come together in public places.

Right to Petition

The First Amendment upholds your right to pass around and present a **petition** calling for legal action or other solutions. A petition is a request for change, usually signed by many people who agree that the change is needed. Can you picture a sheet of paper that's four miles long? Well, that sheet of paper helped women win the right to vote in the early 1900s. It was a petition covered with signatures that a team of women spent a year collecting. The signatures supported women's right to vote. This enormous show of support was part of a campaign that led to the passage of the Nineteenth Amendment in 1919, giving women the right to vote.

Today, you can start your own petition online! Since 2011, you can visit the White House Web site "We the People" to browse open petitions and add your name to support them. It also lets you start your own petition. Once a petition gets enough online support, the government might review it and respond.

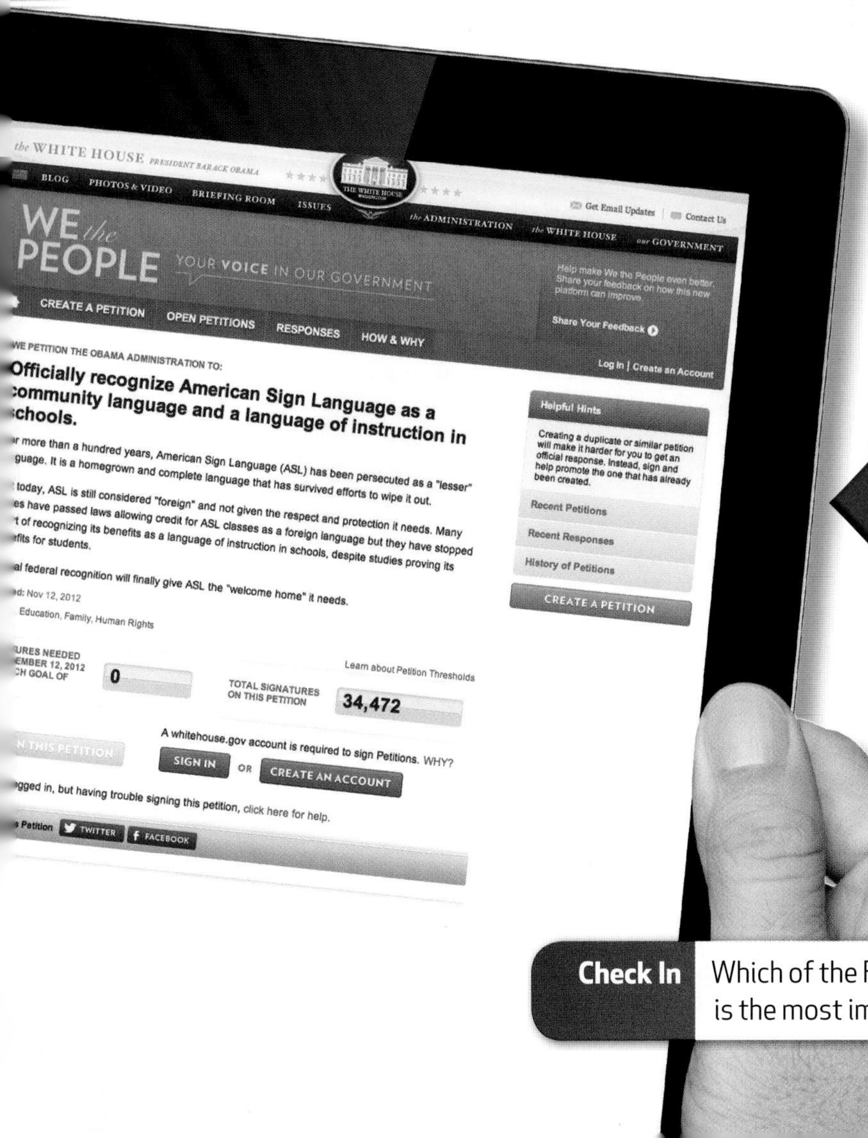

Then James Madison was aware that the British had held the right to petition since 1689, so he made sure the First Amendment gave Americans the same right in the United States.

Now Online petitions make petitioning easy. This petition (left) on the "We the People" Web site, proposes having sign language as an accepted language in schools and other places. You can see they gathered more than 34,000 virtual signatures!

Check In Which of the First Amendment's five freedoms is the most important to you? Explain why.

GENRE Reference Article

Read to find out about Amendments Two through Ten.

Know Your Rights

by Bryon Cahill

2 Bear Arms

The Second Amendment defines the right of **militias,** or local citizens trained to defend their community, to have arms, or weapons. This amendment made sure that citizens could defend themselves if the government ever tried to take away people's rights. Under certain conditions, it's legal for citizens to buy guns in stores like the one shown here.

The Other Nine Amendments

You've learned how important the First Amendment is, but that doesn't mean the others aren't important, too. Amendments Two through Ten safeguard our homes and communities, protect people who are accused of crimes, and limit the federal government's power.

3 Shelter Soldiers

The Third Amendment will probably seem pretty strange to you. It says the government cannot force Americans to feed and shelter soldiers in their homes. Believe it or not, in the days of the American Revolution, this was a problem. Back then, British soldiers could come into colonists' homes and demand food and shelter. Fortunately, this isn't an issue anymore.

4 Search & Seizure

The Fourth Amendment says that no one should face unreasonable search and **seizure.** *Seizure* is the taking of someone's possessions. So unless police or government officials have a good reason—and permission from a judge—they can't force their way into your home to search for evidence. However, in some places, school officials can have students' lockers searched as a safety measure. That's what's happening in the photo above.

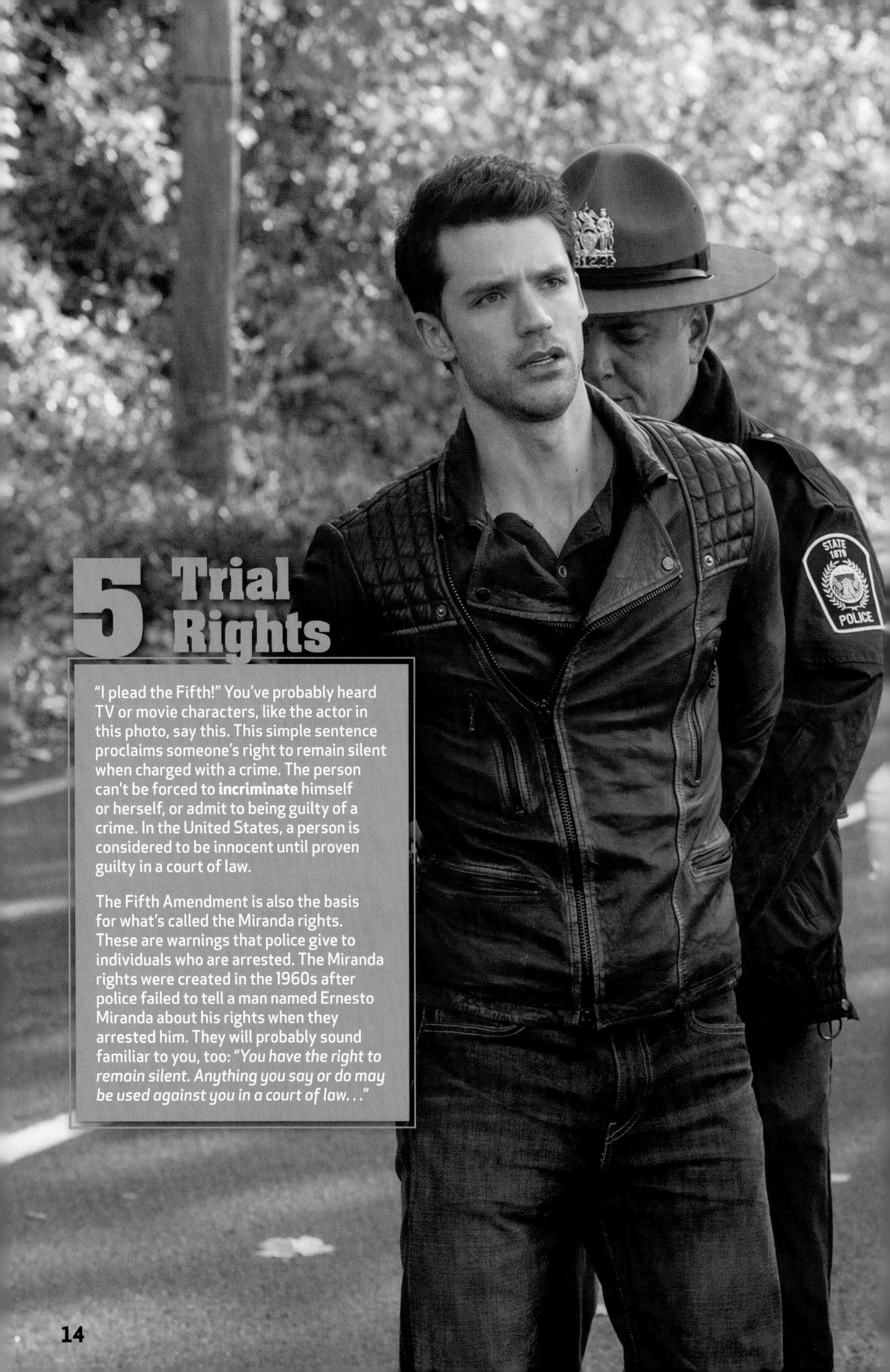

5 Trial Rights

"I plead the Fifth!" You've probably heard TV or movie characters, like the actor in this photo, say this. This simple sentence proclaims someone's right to remain silent when charged with a crime. The person can't be forced to **incriminate** himself or herself, or admit to being guilty of a crime. In the United States, a person is considered to be innocent until proven guilty in a court of law.

The Fifth Amendment is also the basis for what's called the Miranda rights. These are warnings that police give to individuals who are arrested. The Miranda rights were created in the 1960s after police failed to tell a man named Ernesto Miranda about his rights when they arrested him. They will probably sound familiar to you, too: *"You have the right to remain silent. Anything you say or do may be used against you in a court of law. . ."*

6 Speedy Trial

The Sixth Amendment is about court trials. In the United States, citizens have the right to a speedy and public trial. A speedy trial means a person accused of a crime is not locked away in a jail cell for a long time before his or her trial.

While being tried, people have the right to have a lawyer argue their case. If they cannot afford a lawyer, they are assigned one for free.

7 Jury Trial

In colonial days, judges worked for the British king. They didn't care about the colonists who were on trial, and they passed harsh sentences. Thanks to the Seventh Amendment, you have the right to a trial by jury, like the one shown here, and to decisions made by 12 adult citizens.

8 Punishment

"Let the punishment fit the crime!" This famous saying helps us understand the Eighth Amendment, which proclaims that no punishment should be "excessive" or "cruel and unusual." That means that the harshness of the punishment should match the seriousness of the crime.

The Eighth Amendment has caused some disagreement over the years. Some people, like those in this photo, say that the death penalty is cruel and unusual punishment, and they argue that no one in the United States should ever be put to death as a punishment.

9 Additional Rights

The Ninth Amendment promises that other rights not expressly stated in the Bill of Rights are still covered. Some of these include the right to travel freely, the right to marry, and the right to raise and educate children the way we choose. The parents of the students in this photo have chosen to send their children to a public school.

10 State Laws

The Tenth Amendment says that each state has the power to make laws that are not covered by the Constitution. For example, a state can pass its own laws about driving a car, getting married, and starting a business. So if you don't like one state's laws, maybe you can move to a different state!

Check In How do Amendments Two through Ten protect American citizens?

GENRE Poetry **Read to find out** how a poem summarizes the Bill of Rights.

Rapping on Rights

illustrated by John Haslam

Chorus

It's the Bill of Rights, it's the bill of your rights.
It's time to take your knowledge up to unfamiliar heights.
The thrill of your life, just like riding a bike.
You're never, never, never going to forget the Bill of Rights.

Verse 1

The right to free speech and religion and press
Is what you get with the First Amendment.
Amendment Number Two grants the right to bear arms,
Which makes some people content.

The government can't force you to house and feed a soldier,
Says Amendment Number Three.
Amendment Number Four we adore says, without a warrant,
Your stuff can't be searched or seized.

A *warrant* is a document from a judge letting police or government officials search a person or place.

Verse 2

Amendment Number Five says the court can't try you
With evidence they already used.
It also says that nobody can make you self-incriminate.
You're allowed to stay silent if you choose.

When you *self-incriminate*, you give information that makes you look guilty.

Amendment Number Six won't let the criminal clock tick.
The rights of the accused continue here, and then
Amendment Number Seven gives you one plus eleven:
A right to a trial by a jury of your peers.

Peers are people from your own community who are your equals.

If it's cruel and unusual punishment,
It's ruled out by Amendment Eight.
Amendment Number Nine says that other rights are fine,
And Ten gives the rest to the states.

Check In How does this poem help you remember important things about the Bill of Rights?

GENRE Social Studies Article

Read to find out how three students fought for freedom of speech nearly 50 years ago.

WE PROTEST

by Bryon Cahill

^ During the 1960s and 1970s, many American soldiers fought in the war in Vietnam.

TAKING A STAND

What do you feel strongly about? Are you passionate enough about your beliefs to risk being suspended from school for them? In 1965, three students from Des Moines, Iowa, did just that when they stood up for what they believed, even though they were punished for it.

At the time, the United States was taking part in a civil war between North and South Vietnam in Southeast Asia. The United States was fighting to support South Vietnam, but a lot of Americans felt that our soldiers shouldn't be fighting and dying in another nation's war. Two high school students named John Tinker and Christopher Eckhardt and John's younger sister, junior high school student Mary Beth Tinker, opposed the war and wanted it to end. But what could they do to express their opinions?

They had an idea. They would protest the war by wearing black armbands with peace symbols (like the symbol shown to the left). The armbands would express that these teens wanted peace, not war. Unfortunately, expressing their ideas created a lot of trouble for the students!

YOU'RE SUSPENDED!

Even before it took place, word of the students' planned armband protest spread. School officials feared the armbands would be **disruptive**, or distracting to others. Some war protests of the time were loud and active. For example, groups of young men sometimes protested the war by burning their draft cards, which were issued by the government and used to enlist men in the military. However, the protest in Des Moines was planned to be a quiet and peaceful one.

Even so, the principals from local schools decided before the protest happened that any student wearing an armband must take it off or be suspended. Some teachers feared that if students could wear black armbands for this cause, other students would start wearing armbands of other colors to protest all sorts of issues.

The next day the students came to school wearing the armbands. They were careful not to let the protest disrupt

John and Mary Beth Tinker made history. They took a silent stand for what they believed in. Even today, Mary Beth Tinker gives talks in support of free speech.

their classes. School officials asked the students to remove them, but they refused and were suspended. As a result, the students' parents decided to sue the school system. And for the rest of the year some teachers and students **harassed**, or bothered, the protesters. They claimed the armbands supported the enemy in the war, not U.S. soldiers, but that wasn't the protesters' intention. The students wearing armbands simply wanted peace for both sides and an end to the war.

FREE SPEECH WINS!

Finally, the case went to trial. At first, local courts ruled that the schools had the right to ban the armbands. Still, the students and their families believed in the right to free speech and did not give up. In 1968, the case went all the way to the U.S. Supreme Court.

The Court looked at all sides of this issue. In the past, school officials had allowed students to wear symbols that expressed political opinions, such as buttons supporting people running for office. Even though many people disagreed with their stand against the war, these students still had the right to express their views in a peaceful manner.

The Supreme Court judges made their decision. They agreed with the students and their parents. They ruled that the First Amendment protects the students' right to express their opinion against the Vietnam War by wearing the armbands. Even if an opinion is unpopular, they argued, the First Amendment allows for its peaceful expression. The case, called *Tinker v. Des Moines Independent School Board,* became an important Court decision that protected students' rights in the United States.

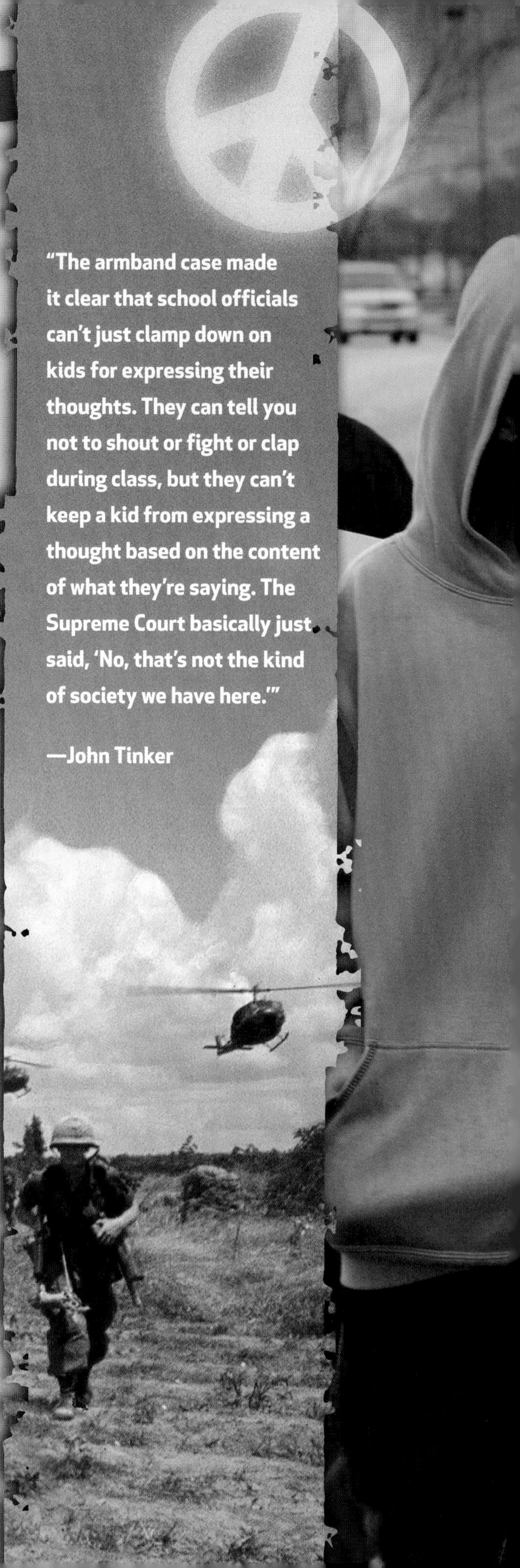

"The armband case made it clear that school officials can't just clamp down on kids for expressing their thoughts. They can tell you not to shout or fight or clap during class, but they can't keep a kid from expressing a thought based on the content of what they're saying. The Supreme Court basically just said, 'No, that's not the kind of society we have here.'"

—John Tinker

Students today are free to protest about important issues such as global warming.

Check In Why is the *Tinker* case important for students today?

GENRE Narrative Nonfiction

Read to find out how freedom of the press helped end slavery in the United States.

A Book That CHANGED THE NATION

by Debbie Nevins
illustrated by Tristan Elwell

From 1861 to 1865, the Civil War raged between Southern and Northern states. This war was about the rights of states, including the right to allow slavery. Ten years earlier, in 1851, Harriet Beecher Stowe had written *Uncle Tom's Cabin*, a novel about Southern slavery. Even though slavery was not legal in the North at that time, many Northerners did not oppose slavery in the South. By describing the cruelty of slavery, Stowe's novel helped change this attitude. Stowe's strong beliefs—and freedom of the press—changed history.

One crisp, autumn evening in Brunswick, Maine, Calvin Stowe came home to find his wife in a fury.

"Oh Calvin, I saw such a dreadful thing today!" Harriet said, slamming a pot lid onto the stove. She took out some onions and began chopping with great force. "It was a poster in town, saying Congress has approved the Fugitive Slave Law."

Passed on September 18, 1850, this law required everyone to help catch **fugitive** slaves—enslaved people who had run away to escape their owners. Anyone who refused could be fined $1,000 (an enormous sum of money in those days) and jailed for six months. Those who turned in fugitive slaves were often paid for their efforts, and even free African Americans were not safe from this law. Some were captured under this law, sent to the South, and enslaved there. They had no legal right to plead their case or to prove their freedom.

"It is a shameful, wicked law, Calvin," Harriet said, waving her kitchen knife in the air. "It forces us to support an immoral, unjust system. It put me in such a disagreeable state that I rushed home and wrote a letter about it to Isabella."

"Well, dear wife, you do wield a mighty knife—I mean, pen," Calvin said. "Your sister-in-law has remarked before about the power of your words."

Harriet mailed her letter and waited eagerly for her sister-in-law's response. A few days later it came. In her letter Isabella Beecher declared: "Now, Hattie, if I could use a pen as you can, I would write something that would make this whole nation feel what an accursed thing slavery is."

Posters like these were pasted to the walls of buildings. The poster on the left warns free blacks that they may be in danger of being kidnapped and turned over to slaveholders. The poster on the right offers a reward for a fugitive slave.

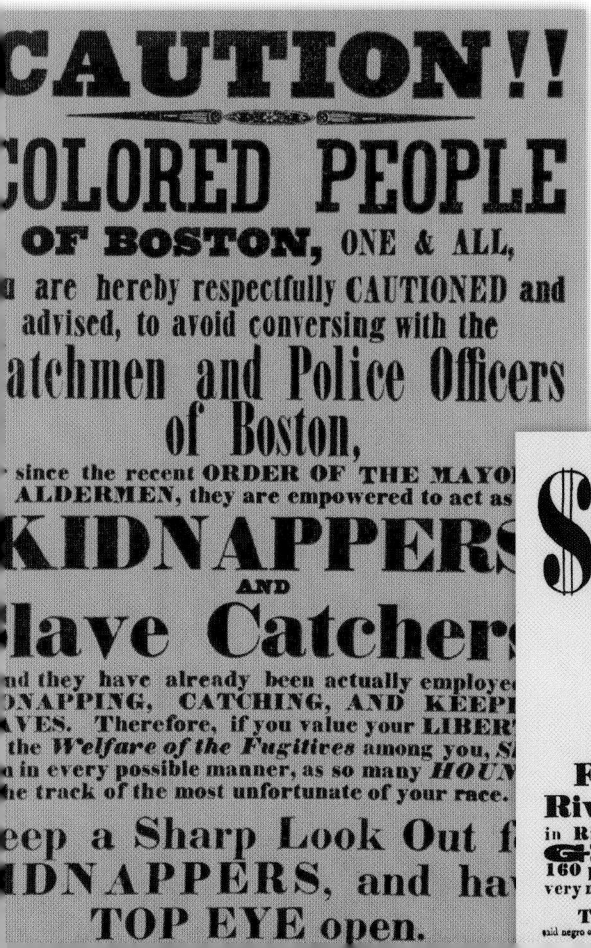

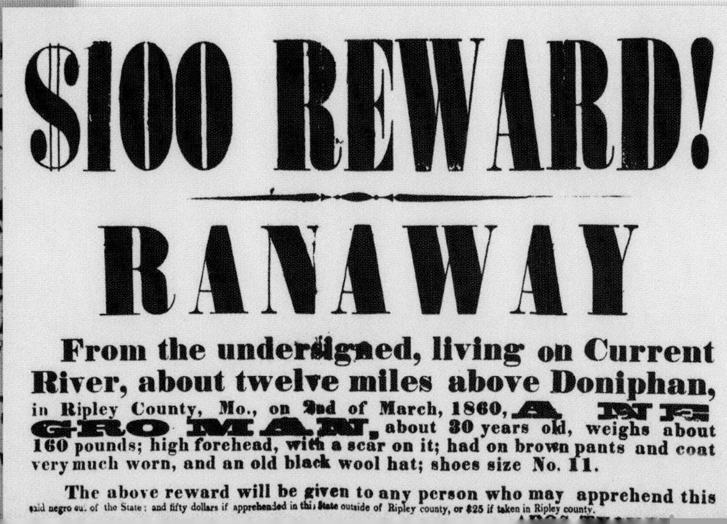

Fugitive slaves cross a river in Virginia. Their wagon holds everything they own.

Boys as young as this one were bought and sold in slave auctions.

Harriet read Isabella's letter aloud to her family. Jumping to her feet, she exclaimed, "I *will* write something." She and Calvin were **abolitionists**, people who wanted to abolish, or ban, slavery. They lived in the North, and every year, hundreds—perhaps thousands—of fugitive slaves fled to Northern states in search of freedom.

A few weeks later while sitting in church, Harriet recalled what she had read about the treatment of slaves, including the severe whippings they sometimes received. After church she rushed home and wrote a fictional passage about an old slave being whipped. When she read it aloud to her children, one of them cried, "Oh Mama! Slavery is the most cruel thing in the world!"

That passage grew into *Uncle Tom's Cabin.* The book tells the story of two enslaved people, good-hearted Uncle Tom and brave Eliza, who work on a **plantation**, or farm, in the Southern

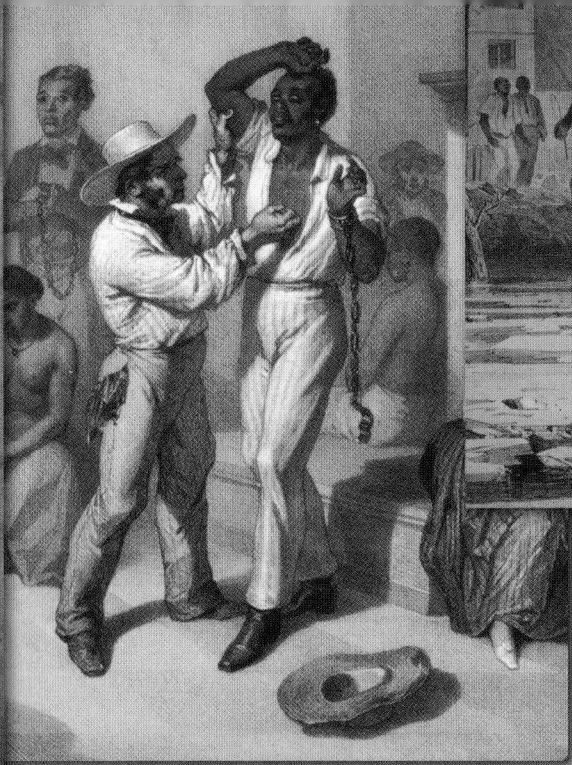

In the book, the characters Eliza and Harry escape their owners and run to freedom.

This illustration is from the book *Uncle Tom's Cabin*. In it, Uncle Tom is being sold at a slave auction.

state of Kentucky. Eliza finds out that the slave owner intends to sell two slaves to pay his debts—one is Tom and the other is Eliza's four-year-old son Harry. Terrified of losing her child, she flees with Harry across the half-frozen Ohio River with slave hunters chasing close behind them. Meanwhile, Tom is sold and must leave his wife and children, never to see them again. A cruel man, Simon Legree, buys Tom, torments him, and eventually kills him. As he lies dying, Tom still manages to forgive his master.

Uncle Tom's Cabin became a best seller in the United States and all over the world. Translated into more than 60 languages, it broke sales records everywhere. Readers were shaken by the descriptions of slavery, and Harriet's words brought them to tears. The story made people cry, but it also made them think. Its forceful message caused many readers to change their minds about slavery, or to strengthen their beliefs against it.

As the outcry against slavery grew, so did conflict between the Northern and Southern states. In 1861, this conflict led to the Civil War. Slavery was one of the issues that fueled the four-year-long war.

Legend has it that Harriet met President Abraham Lincoln in Washington, D.C., in 1862, when the Civil War between the North and South was raging. Some people say that when Lincoln met Harriet, he said, "So you're the little woman who made this great war." Lincoln was referring to the fact that with her book, Harriet had stirred people to fight against slavery.

A poster advertises *Uncle Tom's Cabin*, which was called the most popular book of its day.

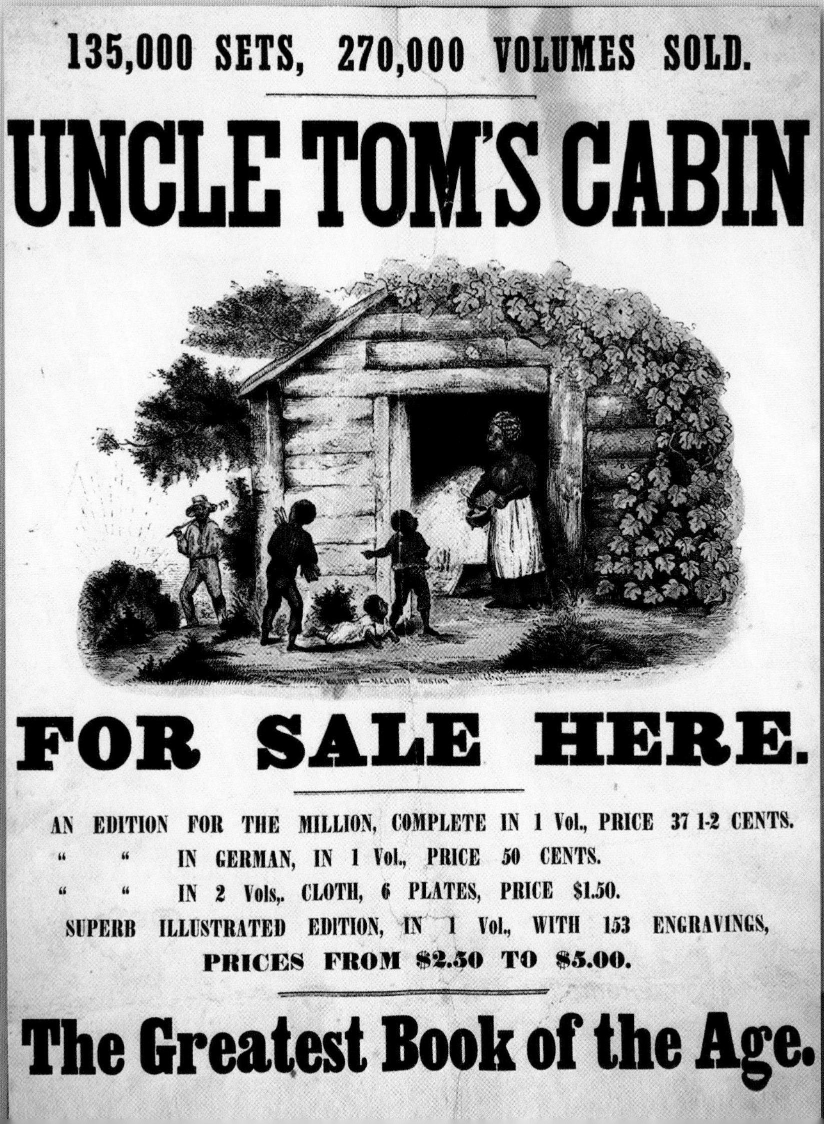

Abraham Lincoln fought very hard to persuade other people in government to support the Emancipation Proclamation.

On January 1, 1863, Harriet attended a concert in Boston to celebrate Lincoln's signing of the Emancipation Proclamation, a document that said that all slaves in Southern states were free. At the concert, audience members spotted Harriet sitting in the balcony. A cheer rose up, "Harriet Beecher Stowe! Harriet Beecher Stowe! Harriet Beecher Stowe!" Harriet stood and waved, her bonnet toppling from her head and tears streaming down her cheeks. She understood the crowd's joy. It was all about the power of words and ideas to sway a nation—and the power of the freedom of the press.

Later in her life, Harriet Beecher Stowe taught freed slaves how to read and write.

"It's a matter of taking the side of the weak against the strong, something the best people have always done."

—Harriet Beecher Stowe

Check In How did *Uncle Tom's Cabin* change people's minds about slavery?

Discuss

1. Tell about some of the ways you think the six selections in this book are linked.

2. Why are the freedoms protected by the Bill of Rights so important to the way people live in the United States?

3. How does the *Tinker* case help you understand the importance of freedom of speech?

4. Why do you think many of the amendments in the Bill of Rights deal with the rights of those who have been accused of a crime?

5. What do you still want to know about why the Bill of Rights was written and how it affects the way we live today?